2022
Toronto

The Restaurant Enthusiast's Discriminating Guide

Andrew Delaplaine

Andrew Delaplaine is the Food Enthusiast.
When he's not playing tennis,
he dines anonymously
at the Publisher's (considerable) expense.

James Cubby – Senior Editor

The Restaurant Enthusiast's
Discriminating Guide

Table of Contents

Introduction

Everyone loves Toronto, or so it seems, as it's the one of the most multi-culturally diverse cities in the world and the most populous city in Canada with almost 3 million residents.

A melting pot of cultures, flavors, and people, with over 140 languages spoken make Toronto a unique destination with its thriving culture, dining, and nightlife.

With all these different cultures represented, it's no wonder festivals abound here and there's a festival for every neighborhood and ethnic group and if you're a festival fan, then visit Toronto during the summer months as there are a dozen or more festivals scheduled every weekend.

If you haven't visited the thriving city of Toronto then it's time to plan your trip, as it is now bigger than Chicago. While records say that Toronto has 301 days of sunshine, the fall is also a great time to visit to experience the amazing autumn foliage and

Oktoberfest.
But just because the winters can be brutal, don't discount Toronto's winter season since it becomes a winter wonderland bustling with chilly sports like cross-country skiing and ice skating – there are 52 outdoor skating rinks in the city.

There are many reasons to visit Toronto, just ask a proud local who just might share some of the reasons that their city is ranked as the world's fourth most livable city.

One of the accolades that you might hear from locals is the fact that Toronto ranks second as the world's most business competitive global city.

There's certainly competition in the dining community as Toronto boasts more than 8,000 restaurants so you're certain to find a dining spot suitable for your tastes and pocketbook.

Yes, Toronto's food scene can certainly give any city in the world stiff competition. If you're looking for a good cup of coffee and prefer an indie coffee shop instead of the overrated Starbucks chain, then Toronto is your city.

Toronto is also a favorite destination of the film industry as it's North America's third largest city for movie production.

It that's not enough to convince you to visit Toronto, then check out the wealth of attractions like the exciting theme parks, zoos, gardens, and golf courses and be prepared to fall in love.

THE A to Z LISTINGS

Ridiculously Extravagant
Sensible Alternatives
Quality Bargain Spots

416 SNACK BAR
181 Bathurst St, Toronto, 416-364-9320
www.416snackbar.com
CUISINE: Tapas
DRINKS: Full Bar
SERVING: Dinner/Late Night
PRICE RANGE: $$
This hip tapas-style eatery offers an ever-changing menu including everything from Jamaican patties to charcuterie. Favorites include: Fresh mango salad.

ACTINOLITE
971 Ossington Ave, Toronto, 416-962-8943
www.actinoliterestaurant.com
CUISINE: Canadian
DRINKS: Full Bar
SERVING: Dinner; closed Sun & Mon
PRICE RANGE: $$$$
This sleek eatery offers fixed price & chef's menus of locally sourced New Canadian fare. Menu favorites include: Pork Shoulder appetizer glazed in apple cider

and Marinated Veal T-bone served on creamed spinach puree. Nice wine list.

Very hard to see the details because it's so dark in Akira Back, but it's stunning.

AKIRA BACK
80 Blue Jays Way, Toronto, 437-800-5967
https://www.akirabacktoronto.com/
CUISINE: Japanese / Asian Fusion
DRINKS: Full Bar
SERVING: Dinner
PRICE RANGE: $$$$
NEIGHBORHOOD: Entertainment District, Downtown Core
Upscale eatery serving creative Japanese cuisine featuring an interior design that has to be seen. If I were the chef here, I might start thinking people were

coming to look at the charcoal black walls or the black marble columns or the gold trim accenting the jaw-dropping blue graphic ceiling, rather than eat my food. I'm sure Akira, the Michelin-starred chef who gives his name to this place, has nothing to worry about. Not as long as he continues to serve up the high level of sushi that he does. My Favorites: Botain Shrimp and Jidori Chicken. There's a 48-hour Wagyu Short Rib that's quite incredible. I was rolling my eyes after the first bite. Try their Tuna and Mushroom Pizza if you're looking for something a little less serious. A lot of work went into this place, not just in the front of the house, but the kitchen as well. Professionals working at their highest level. Reservations recommended.

Entry to Akira Back is modern & sleek.

ALOETTE
163 Spadina Ave. 1st Floor, Toronto, 416-260-3444
https://aloetterestaurant.com/
CUISINE: French
DRINKS: Full Bar
SERVING: Lunch & Dinner

PRICE RANGE: $$$
NEIGHBORHOOD: Queen Street West, Entertainment District, Downtown Core
Tiny but chic eatery offering a creative menu of French comfort food and classics. It's very narrow, with bar stools on one side and little booths on the other. There's barely room to squeeze by when both sides are packed. But it's worth it. My Favorites: Roasted Cod and Beef Tartare. Varied cocktail list. Vegetarian options. Homemade desserts.

ASCARI ENOTECA
1111 Queen St E, Toronto, 416-792-4157
www.ascari.ca/
CUISINE: Italian
DRINKS: Full Bar
SERVING: Dinner
PRICE RANGE: $$$
NEIGHBORHOOD: Leslieville

This popular spot with a racing-themed décor offers a menu of authentic Italian cuisine using local and sustainable foods. The wines are also organic and local. The pasta is made on the premises. Menu favorites include: Roasted Cauliflower Fettuccine and Chicken Liver Mousse.

AUBERGE DU POMMIER
4150 Yonge St, Toronto, 416-222-2220
www.aubergedupommier.com
CUISINE: French
DRINKS: Full Bar
SERVING: Lunch, Dinner; closed Sun
PRICE RANGE: $$$$
NEIGHBORHOOD: North of York Mills
This sophisticated French restaurant offers an impressive menu including a 5-course tasting menu (highly recommended). The wine list is quite

impressive. Favorites include: Foie gras mousse and Quail & Lobster.

BANNOCK
401 Bay St, Toronto, 416-861-6996
www.bannockrestaurant.com
CUISINE: Canadian
DRINKS: Full Bar
SERVING: Breakfast, Lunch & Dinner
PRICE RANGE: $$
NEIGHBORHOOD: Downtown Core
This casual eatery offers a Canadian-inspired menu featuring global dishes.
Menu favorites include: Chicken potpie and Duck Poutine pizza.

BAR CHEF
472 Queen Street W, Toronto, 416-868-4800
www.barchef.com
CUISINE: French/American
DRINKS: Full Bar
SERVING: Dinner
PRICE RANGE: $$$
NEIGHBORHOOD: Alexandra Park, Queen Street West
Intimate, dimly lit bar offering (with pretty steep prices) an amazing selection of housemade bitters that infuse so many of their creative cocktails. Tried the Vanilla Hickory Smoked Manhattan and it's delish. Mojito fans should try the Coconut Mojito.

BAR ISABEL
797 College St, Toronto, 416-532-2222
https://barisabel.com/
CUISINE: Spanish
DRINKS: Full Bar
SERVING: Dinner
PRICE RANGE: $$$$
NEIGHBORHOOD: Bickford Park, Little Italy
Upscale eatery with Spanish-inspired menu. Favorites: Roasted Bone Marrow and Grilled Octopus. Their Sourdough loaf is a must-try. Creative desserts. Reservations recommended.

BAR RAVAL
505 College St, Toronto, 647-344-8001
www.thisisbarraval.com

CUISINE: Spanish/Tapas
DRINKS: Full Bar
SERVING: Breakfast, Lunch, Dinner
PRICE RANGE: $$$
NEIGHBORHOOD: Little Italy, Palmerston

Relaxed European-style bar similar to a Barcelona style pintxos & tapas bar with a small menu of dishes like octopus and bay scallops. The interior is a mashup of Gaudi-style whimsicalities. Open 8 a.m. till past midnight. The morning is nice because they have great coffee and sweet & savory pastries. Galician tinned seafood specialties in the afternoon are nice, as well as the charcuterie boards, and the Squid, Artichokes and Romesco. Nice selection of desserts like Spanish pie.

BIAGIO RISTORANTE
155 King St E, Toronto, ON, 416-366-4040
www.biagioristorante.ca
CUISINE: Italian
DRINKS: Full Bar
SERVING: Lunch & Dinner; closed Sun
PRICE RANGE: $$

NEIGHBORHOOD: St. Lawrence
This beautiful upscale ristorante offers a menu of delicious Italian cuisine. Menu favorites include: Homemade tagliolini with brandy lamb and Grilled veal tenderloin. Their special creamy cheesecake is wrapped in puff pastry served with fresh berries. Impressive 1,500 label wine list.

CAFÉ AT THE GLADSTONE HOTEL
1214 Queen St W, Toronto, 416-531-4635
www.gladstonehotel.com/food-drink/
CUISINE: Fusion
DRINKS: Full Bar
SERVING: Breakfast, Lunch & Dinner
PRICE RANGE: $$
NEIGHBORHOOD: Queen West
Located at the Gladstone Hotel, this popular café serves great coffee and features Chef Mario Paz's creative menu of Toronto classics. Great place for breakfast, lunch or dinner and is a favorite brunch destination. Nice wine list.

CAFÉ AT DRAKE HOTEL
1150 Queen Street W, Toronto, 416-531-5042
www.thedrakehotel.ca/dining
CUISINE: Canadian
DRINKS: Full Bar
SERVING: Breakfast, Brunch & Lunch
PRICE RANGE: $$
NEIGHBORHOOD: West Queen West/Beaconsfield Village
This neighborhood eatery is a popular breakfast destination. Favorites include the blueberry scones and Drake burger. Great coffee and home of the best hangover cure in town.

CAFÉ BELONG
550 Bayview Ave, Toronto, 416-901-8234
www.cafebelong.ca/
CUISINE: Cafe
DRINKS: Full Bar
SERVING: Brunch, Lunch & Dinner
PRICE RANGE: $$$

NEIGHBORHOOD: East York
This popular café offers a seasonal menu but is most popular for its brunches. Here you'll find great eggs benedict, pancakes, French toast, all sustainable and locally sourced. Menu favorites include: Cedar Scented Yorkshire Valley Chicken and Muskoka Battterd Great Lakes Perch. Dinner menu divided into three categories: Cold Kitchen, Communal, and Hot Kitchen. Impressive cocktail menu.

CAFÉ BOULUD
FOUR SEASONS HOTEL
60 Yorkville Ave, Toronto, 416-963-6000
www.cafeboulud.com
CUISINE: Cafe
DRINKS: Full Bar
SERVING: Breakfast, Lunch & Dinner
PRICE RANGE: $$$$
NEIGHBORHOOD: Yorkville
Located inside the Four Seasons Hotel, this loftlike space offers a menu of Mediterranean-inspired fare. Menu favorites include: Crispy Duck Egg appetizer and Terrine of Lamb Leg. Impressive list of wines.

CANOE RESTAURANT & BAR
66 Wellington St W, Toronto, 416-364-0054
www.canoerestaurant.com
CUISINE: Canadian
DRINKS: Full Bar
SERVING: Lunch & Dinner; closed Sat & Sun
PRICE RANGE: $$$$
NEIGHBORHOOD: Financial District

Located on the 54th floor of the TD Bank Tower, this upscale eatery offers incredible views and an impressive menu of Chef John Horne's regional Canadian cuisine. Favorites include: Foie gras and Alberta lamb. Excellent wine pairings. Dessert choices include: chocolate hazelnut torte, the chocolate peanut dessert, and the roasted peaches.

CIBO
522 King Street W, Toronto, 416-504-3939
www.cibowinebar.com
CUISINE: Italian
DRINKS: Full Bar
SERVING: Lunch & Dinner
PRICE RANGE: $$$
NEIGHBORHOOD: King West
This restaurant/wine bar offers a menu of authentic Italian fare. Menu favorites include: Risotto with porcini mushrooms and Arugula & Prosciutto Di Parma with shaved parmigiano reggiano. Popular

Sunday brunch destination with omelette and pizza stations.

DAILO
503 College St, Toronto, 647-341-8882
https://dailoto.com/
CUISINE: Asian
DRINKS: Full Bar
SERVING: Dinner; Closed Mon
PRICE RANGE: $$$
NEIGHBORHOOD: Little Italy
Two-level Asian-themed brasserie with a French/Chinese menu. Favorites: Truffle Fried Rice and Giggie Fish. Creative cocktails.

DREYFUS
96 Harbord St, Toronto, 416-323-1385
https://dreyfustoronto.com/
CUISINE: French
DRINKS: Full Bar
SERVING: Dinner: Closed Sun & Mon
PRICE RANGE: $$$
NEIGHBORHOOD: Downtown
Located in a little brick row house that I particularly like to visit when the weather is cold outside, this cozy French eatery serves simple dishes designed to be shared. (Check the handwritten chalkboard for daily specials—you can't go wrong with them.) Favorites: Steak Tartare and Duck Breast. Excellent cocktails. Reservations are a must and difficult to get.

DYNASTY
69 Yorkville Ave, Toronto, 416-923-3323
www.dynastyyorkville.com
CUISINE: Dim Sum

DRINKS: Full Bar
SERVING: Lunch & Dinner
PRICE RANGE: $$$
NEIGHBORHOOD: Yorkville
This upscale eatery offers an extensive menu of traditional fare and dim sum. Favorites include: Dynasty Peking Duck and Szechuan Orange Peel Beef. If you're a fan of dim sum then you'll love this place.

EDULIS
169 Niagara St, Toronto, 416-703-4222
www.edulisrestaurant.com
CUISINE: Spanish

DRINKS: Full Bar
SERVING: Dinner; closed Mon & Tues
PRICE RANGE: $$$$
NEIGHBORHOOD: Niagara
This cozy eatery offers a seasonal menu of fresh local ingredients. There are two choices here: a 5-course tasting menu and a 7-course tasting menu. Good wine selection and tasty fresh baked bread. Favorites include: Sockeye salmon and Lamb stewed with seasonal vegetables.

EL CATRIN
18 Tank House Lane, Toronto, 416-203-2121
www.elcatrin.ca
CUISINE: Mexican/Tapas
DRINKS: Full Bar
SERVING: Lunch, Dinner
PRICE RANGE: $$$
NEIGHBORHOOD: Distillery District
Trendy eatery in a cavernous space offering upscale Mexican fare. There are some 45 buildings that make up the Distillery District, which constitutes the biggest collection of Victorian "industrial architecture" in North America. (Some of the oldest buildings go back to the 1850s.) The cobblestone streets are home to all kinds of artisans, artists' studios, jewelry shops, galleries (Arta, Thompson Landry and others). El Catrin is one of the best dining options in the District. Nice selection of tequilas. Favorites: Fish and shrimp tacos.

EL TROMPO
277 Augusta Ave, Toronto, 416-260-0097

www.eltrompo.ca
CUISINE: Mexican
DRINKS: Full Bar
SERVING: Dinner; closed Mon
PRICE RANGE: $$
NEIGHBORHOOD: Kensington Market
This is basically a taco bar with a menu of authentic Mexican fare. Favorites include: Spicy Tinga Chicken tacos (4 tacos per order). Tasty margaritas.

ELLA'S UNCLE
916 Dundas Street West, 416-703-8881

www.ellasuncle.com
WEBSITE DOWN AT PRESS TIME
CUISINE: Coffee Shop
DRINKS: Full Bar
SERVING: Breakfast & Lunch
PRICE RANGE: $$$$
NEIGHBORHOOD: Little Italy
This casual but very busy coffee shop offers a friendly atmosphere for breakfast, lunch or just coffee and dessert. Try the delicious banana bread with chocolate chips. People come here just for the great coffee.

FIGO
295 Adelaide St W, Toronto, 647-748-3446
www.figotoronto.com
CUISINE: Italian
DRINKS: Full Bar
SERVING: Lunch, Dinner; Brunch on Sat & Sun
PRICE RANGE: $$$
NEIGHBORHOOD: Entertainment District, Downtown Core
Sleek Italian eatery with a pastel on white interior design offering creative dishes like Ricotta Pancakes (for brunch) and house-made ricotta, wood-fired pizzas, and made-from-scratch pastas. It's nicely located half a block away from the Lightbox, so very convenient for those attending the Toronto Film Festival.

FOXLEY BISTRO
207 Ossington Ave, Toronto, 416-534-8520
https://foxleybistro.com

CUISINE: Asian Fusion/Tapas
DRINKS: Full Bar
SERVING: Dinner; closed Sun
PRICE RANGE: $$$
NEIGHBORHOOD: Little Portugal
This cozy eatery offers a menu of Asian and Pan-Latin cuisine. Favorites include: Sea scallops ceviche and Lamb & duck prosciutto dumplings. Most dishes are served tapas style.

GIA
1214 Dundas St W, Toronto, 416-535-8888
https://giarestaurant.ca/
CUISINE: Vegetarian / Vegan
DRINKS: Full Bar
SERVING: Dinner; Closed Sun
PRICE RANGE: $$
NEIGHBORHOOD: Little Portugal, Beaconsfield Village, Dufferin Grove

Healthy eatery offering a menu of plant-based and vegetarian mains. The bricks painted white and the marble tables set the tone for an upscale place serving what these days is called a "plant forward" menu. Truth is, you've never tasted mushrooms as good as these. Produce is supplied by the best in local purveyors. My Favorites: Spaghetti Bolognese and Risotto. Their fresh homemade pasta is always a special treat here because of the succulent toppings and sauces they so lovingly prepare to go with it.

JACOBS & CO STEAKHOUSE
12 Brant St, Toronto, 416-366-0200
www.jacobssteakhouse.com
CUISINE: Steakhouse
DRINKS: Full Bar
SERVING: Dinner
PRICE RANGE: $$$$

NEIGHBORHOOD: King West
This upscale eatery and piano bar offers an elegant atmosphere for dining. Creative menu featuring a variety of meats and seafood. The restaurant also features a raw bar. Favorites include the A5 Black Tajima or Snake River Farms' Wagyu. Save room for their infamous Flourless Almond & Coconut Cake. Impressive wine list.

Various cuts aging at Jacobs Steakhouse

LADY MARMALADE
265 Broadview Ave, Toronto, 647-351-7645
www.ladymarmalade.ca
CUISINE: Mexican
DRINKS: No Booze
SERVING: Breakfast & Lunch
PRICE RANGE: $$
NEIGHBORHOOD: Leslieville

Here you'll find a globally inspired menu with a definite Mexican flavor. This is a popular spot for breakfast with a menu that includes dishes like: Aged white cheddar & spinach waffles and Lady Marmalade "bennies" (their unique version of Eggs Benedict). The kitchen uses locally sourced foods and offers gluten-free choices.

LA FENICE RISTORANTE
319 King St W, Toronto, 416-585-2377
www.lafenice.ca
CUISINE: Italian
DRINKS: Full Bar
SERVING: Dinner

PRICE RANGE: $$$
NEIGHBORHOOD: Entertainment District
After more than 25 years, this Italian eatery still packs the house. The menu offers a variety of classic Italian dishes as well as excellent seafood. Favorites include: Spaghetti with shrimp, rapini and pancetta. Nice wine list. Gluten-free options available.

LAHORE TIKKA HOUSE
1365 Gerrard St E, Toronto, 416-406-1668
www.lahoretikkahouse.com
CUISINE: Indian/Pakistani
DRINKS: No Booze
SERVING: Lunch & Dinner
PRICE RANGE: $$
NEIGHBORHOOD: Leslieville
This colorful Pakistani eatery offers a menu of traditional modern North Indian cuisine with sizzling BBQ and curries. Orders are placed at the counter but almost as soon as you're seated your food is served. Note: food is served on Styrofoam plates and eaten with plastic utensils. This place is usually busy and there's often a wait.

LAI WAH HEEN
METROPOLITAN HOTEL
108 Chestnut St, Toronto, 416-977-9899
www.laiwahheen.com
CUISINE: Dim Sum
DRINKS: Full Bar
SERVING: Dinner
PRICE RANGE: $$$
NEIGHBORHOOD: Downtown Core

Located in the Metropolitan Hotel, this upscale eatery offers a creative menu of Chinese cuisine and Dim Sum. Popular dishes include: Shrimp dumplings, Beef rice rolls, and Siu Mai.

LAZY DAISY'S CAFÉ
1515 Gerrard St E, Toronto, 647-341-4070
www.lazydaisyscafe.ca
CUISINE: Cafe
DRINKS: Full Bar
SERVING: Breakfast & Lunch
PRICE RANGE: $$
NEIGHBORHOOD: Leslieville
Comfortable café that is a favorite among locals. Great menu features local, organic, farm-to-table ingredients like free-range egg & cheddar cheese on a biscuit, Mennonite smoked bacon. There's also a grilled cheese sandwich made really special with the addition of slow-roasted pork. Great pizzas and a delicious blueberry cheesecake. They feature events

like Trivia Night every second Wednesday, Family Happy Hour every Saturday and Open Mic Nights.

LE SWAN

892 Queen St W, Toronto, 416-536-4440
https://leswan.ca/
CUISINE: Diner / French
DRINKS: Full Bar
SERVING: Dinner, Lunch & Dinner Fri - Sun
PRICE RANGE: $$$
NEIGHBORHOOD: West Queen West, Trinity Bellwoods

Upscale Art-Deco style French diner serving classics and comfort fare. A step up from typical diners but remaining true to the old-style charm. It's a little confusing, because the food served here makes you feel like this is a French Bistro masquerading as an old-time diner. The food is, how shall I say, elevated beyond typical diner fare, which is why you get Smoked Trout Rillette, Fondue, Sole Meunière and Steak Frites while at the other end of the spectrum, you can also get Pork Chops with applesauce, Chicken Fried Steak and Milkshakes. The crew manning the bar are no slouches either, so you can expect perfectly executed cocktails. I think this is one of the cleverest places in town. Impressive wine list. Reservations recommended.

LOCALE MERCATTO
330 Bay St, Toronto, 416-306-0467
www.mercatto.ca
CUISINE: Italian
DRINKS: Full Bar
SERVING: Breakfast, Lunch &Dinner
PRICE RANGE: $$
NEIGHBORHOOD: Financial District
Part of a mini-chain but it feels like it's a high-end eatery. The menu features Italian classics and creative

specials. Favorites include: Spaghetti Chitarra with octopus and Costatine (Short Ribs). Nice selection of Italian wines and rich desserts.

LUMA
Inside the TIFF Bell
350 King Street W, Toronto, 647-288-4715
www.lumarestaurant.com
CUISINE: Canadian
DRINKS: Full Bar
SERVING: Lunch & Dinner
PRICE RANGE: $$$
NEIGHBORHOOD: Entertainment District

Located on the 2nd floor of the TIFF Bell Lightbox, this eatery offers a menu of creative Canadian cuisine. Favorites include: Chicken Supreme and Octopus salad.
Great desserts like the chocolate parfait.

MAPLE LEAF TAVERN
955 Gerrard Street E, Toronto, 416-465-0955
https://mapleleaftavern.ca/
CUISINE: American (Traditional)
DRINKS: Full Bar
SERVING: Dinner; Closed Mon & Tues
PRICE RANGE: $$$
NEIGHBORHOOD: Midtown East
Built in 1910, this wood-dominated gastropub offers a menu of wood-grilled chops, steaks, fish and other comfort food. This part of Gerrard Street used to be quite rough-and-tumble, but this place has given the area a lot of much-needed class. The comfy booths set the tone, along with the low lighting and cool vibe

you pick up the minute you enter. My Menu Picks: Elk Cheeks and Chestnut Tagliatelle. People rave about the Burger here, but I find too many other things on the menu more interesting, so can't comment. Impressive cocktail list executed by pros. Reservations recommended.

MARBEN
488 Wellington St W, Toronto, 416-979-1990
https://www.marben.ca/
CUISINE: Canadian (New)/Gastropub
DRINKS: Full Bar
SERVING: Lunch & Dinner; Closed Mon
PRICE RANGE: $$$
NEIGHBORHOOD: Wellington Place/Fashion District
Industrial-style eatery offering an eclectic menu of locally sourced cuisine. This was one of the first places in town to do the whole "sustainable" thing,

sourcing produce and meats locally and ensuring that the very best ingredients were used in their dishes. Over time, the place has ripened into a local treasure, where on your first visit you'll feel as at home as if you'd been coming here for years, the way many of their customers have been. Favorites: Black Angus Sirloin and Pork Belly. For groups I suggest the dessert platter (2 ice cream sandwiches, ginger cake and rhubarb & apple crumble). Vegan options. Bespoke cocktails.

MIKU TORONTO
10 Bay St #105, Toronto, 647-347-7347
https://mikutoronto.com/
CUISINE: French/American
DRINKS: Full Bar
SERVING: Dinner
PRICE RANGE: $$$
NEIGHBORHOOD: Harbourfront

Fine-dining Japanese eatery that you enter through the lobby of RBC Waterpark Place. Try their specialty – flame-seared sushi. Try the Aburi sampler for a treat. Menu favorites: Lobster butter-poached, Albacore Tuna and Wakame Tartare. Creative desserts.

MOTIMAHAI
1422 Gerrard St E. Toronto, 416-461-3111
https://www.facebook.com/Motimahal-Restaurants-237074869673477/
CUISINE: Indian
DRINKS: No Booze
SERVING: Lunch & Dinner; closed Tues
PRICE RANGE: $
NEIGHBORHOOD: Entertainment District
This minimal eatery offers a menu of Indian fare. Favorites include: Malai Kofta and Naan with veggie thali.

MOTHER'S DUMPLINGS
421 Spadina Ave, Toronto, 416-217-2008

www.mothersdumplings.com
WEBSITE DOWN AT PRESSTIME
CUISINE: Chinese
DRINKS: Beer & Wine Only
SERVING: Lunch & Dinner
PRICE RANGE: $$
NEIGHBORHOOD: Chinatown
This traditional eatery offers a menu of basic Chinese cuisine and shareable plates. Favorites include: Shumai and Pork & Bok Choy. They offer sweet dumplings for dessert.

MORTON'S, THE STEAKHOUSE
4 Avenue Rd, Toronto, 416-925-0648
www.mortons.com
CUISINE: Steakhouse
DRINKS: Full Bar
SERVING: Dinner
PRICE RANGE: $$$$
NEIGHBORHOOD: The Annex
The infamous Morton's offers its classic menu of aged prime beef, seafood and traditional steakhouse fare. I know it's a chain, but it's still pretty damn good. Favorites include: Center-cut filet mignon and Signature cut prime New York Strip. Save room for their legendary hot chocolate cake.

NU BÜGEL
240 Augusta Ave, Toronto, 647-748-4488
www.nubugel.com

CUISINE: Bagels
DRINKS: Beer & Wine
SERVING: Breakfast & Lunch
PRICE RANGE: $$
NEIGHBORHOOD: Kensington Market
This popular breakfast has creative offerings like a breakfast bagel stuffed with fluffy egg, thin bacon and a hint of cheddar cheese and Smoked trout with horseradish jelly. The bagels are cooked in a wood-burning oven, which gives them a special taste.

OK OK DINER
1128 Queen St E, Toronto, 416-461-2988
www.okokdiner.com/ **WEBSITE DOWN AT PRESSTIME**
CUISINE: Diner
DRINKS: Beer & Wine Only
SERVING: Breakfast & Lunch
PRICE RANGE: $$
NEIGHBORHOOD: Leslieville
This neighborhood diner offers a menu of hearty comfort fare. Like all diners, this is the spot for all-day breakfasts like French Toast covered in peanut butter and banana. Outdoor patio –weather permitting.

OPUS RESTAURANT ON PRINCE ARTHUR
37 Prince Arthur Ave, Toronto, 416-921-3105
www.opusrestaurant.com
CUISINE: Canadian
DRINKS: Full Bar
SERVING: Dinner
PRICE RANGE: $$$$

NEIGHBORHOOD: The Annex
This high-end elegant restaurant offers a menu of creative Canadian cuisine. Favorites include: Jacob's steak and Rack of Lamb. Save room for the Dark chocolate molten cake. Wine list features over 2,500 labels.

PAI
18 Duncan St, Toronto, 416-901-4724
https://paitoronto.com/
CUISINE: Thai
DRINKS: Beer & Wine
SERVING: Lunch & Dinner, Dinner only Mon
PRICE RANGE: $$
NEIGHBORHOOD: Entertainment District, Downtown Core
Casual eatery offering a menu of authentic northern Thai cuisine. This place is so good it was recognized by the Thai government acknowledging the authentic nature of the food served here. The customers seem to

agree, based on the number of times I've been here when the house was packed. My Favorites: Salted Crab & Papaya Salad and Pad Kra Pow with Crispy Pork. Lots of Curry dishes. Thai desserts. Reservations but expect a wait.

PHO HUNG
350 Spadina Ave, Toronto, 416-593-4274
www.phohung.ca
CUISINE: Vietnamese
DRINKS: Beer & Wine
SERVING: Lunch & Dinner
PRICE RANGE: $
NEIGHBORHOOD: Chinatown
This family-run eatery offers up a large menu of authentic Vietnamese cuisine. Favorites include: Curried chicken and pork with rice and Crispy spring rolls. Try the tasty fruit shakes.

PAESE RISTORANTE
3827 Bathurst St, Toronto, 416-631-6585
www.paeseristorante.com
CUISINE: Italian
DRINKS: Full Bar
SERVING: Lunch & Dinner
PRICE RANGE: $$$
NEIGHBORHOOD: Entertainment District
This popular eatery offers a menu of traditional Italian fare. Favorites include: Veal Scaloppini and Italian Ham pizza. Impressive wine list of over 500 labels.

PIZZERIA LIBRETTO
221 Ossington Ave, Toronto, 416-532-8000
www.pizzerialibretto.com
CUISINE: Pizza/Italian
DRINKS: Full Bar
SERVING: Lunch & Dinner

PRICE RANGE: $$
NEIGHBORHOOD: Little Portugal
This popular pizzeria serves pies from a wood-fired-oven. Here you'll find a busy restaurant and delicious authentic Neapolitan pizza. Another favorite is the Homemade sausage and caramelized onion with mozzarella. No reservations.

POSTICINO RISTORANTE
755 The Queensway, Toronto, 416-253-9207
www.posticino.com
CUISINE: Italian
DRINKS: Full Bar
SERVING: Lunch & Dinner
PRICE RANGE: $$
NEIGHBORHOOD: Etobicoke
This Italian eatery offers traditional cuisine in a contemporary setting. They offer a simple 2 page menu featuring pastas, risottos, meat, seafood, and a nice selection of wine.

RICHMOND STATION
1 Richmond St W, Toronto, 647-748-1444
www.richmondstation.ca
CUISINE: Canadian
DRINKS: Full Bar
SERVING: Lunch & Dinner; closed Sun
PRICE RANGE: $$
NEIGHBORHOOD: Downtown Core
Executive chef Carl Heinrich offers a menu of "good, honest cooking". Menu favorites include: Rib-stuffed burger and Kolapore Springs rainbow trout. Co-owned by a "Top Chef Canada" winner, this bustling spot offers a daily menu of seasonal cuisine.

THE RIVIERA
102 Lakeshore Ave, Toronto, 416-203-2152
www.islandriviera.com
CUISINE: Cafe
DRINKS: Full Bar
SERVING: Lunch, Dinner
PRICE RANGE: $$$
NEIGHBORHOOD: Ward's Island

Tourist hangout with small eclectic menu, just a 10-minute ferry ride to Ward's Island. A lot of places out here are closed in the winter, but this eatery, just off the 1.5 mile boardwalk, is open year-round. Menu picks: Nachos and Pulled pork sandwich. Burgers but also vegetarian options.

ROSE AND SONS
176 Dupont St, Toronto, 647-748-3287
www.roseandsons.ca
CUISINE: Comfort Food
DRINKS: Full Bar
SERVING: Breakfast, Lunch & Dinner
PRICE RANGE: $$
NEIGHBORHOOD: The Annex
This eclectic diner equipped with booths and barstools, offers a creative menu of comfort food. Favorites include: Fried chicken & soft 'n sexy grits and Grilled brie cornbread brisket. Save room for

some delicious homemade bread pudding with wild blueberries.

RUTH'S CHRIS STEAK HOUSE
145 Richmond Street W, Toronto, 416-955-1455
www.ruthschris.ca
CUISINE: Steakhouse
DRINKS: Full Bar
SERVING: Dinner
PRICE RANGE: $$$$
NEIGHBORHOOD: Financial District
This popular upscale steakhouse offers a menu of award-winning cuisine featuring a variety of entrees, steaks, seafood and poultry, and delicious desserts. Favorites include: Blue Crab Cakes and Buttercup Shrimp. Extensive wine list.

SANAGAN'S MEAT LOCKER
176 Baldwin St, Toronto, 416-593-9747
www.sanagansmeatlocker.com
CUISINE: Meat Shop
DRINKS: Full Bar
SERVING: Lunch & Dinner
PRICE RANGE: $$
NEIGHBORHOOD: Kensington Market
This old fashioned butcher shop also has a food counter that serves great chicken sandwiches and fries. This is definitely a meat-eaters paradise.

THE SENATOR RESTAURANT
249 Victoria Street, Toronto, 416-364-7517
www.thesenator.com
CUISINE: Diner
DRINKS: Full Bar
SERVING: Breakfast, Lunch & Dinner
PRICE RANGE: $$
NEIGHBORHOOD: Downtown Core
This retro diner offers a menu of classic comfort food. Of course there's breakfast all day so try their Eggs Benedict. Wildly popular in these parts.

SCARAMOUCHE
1 Benvenuto Place, Toronto, 416-961-8011
http://www.scaramoucherestaurant.com/
CUISINE: French
DRINKS: Full Bar
SERVING: Dinner; Closed Sun & Mon
PRICE RANGE: $$$$
NEIGHBORHOOD: South Hill
I always end up getting dragged to the hot and trendy "latest thing" when I visit my deputy editors in Toronto and we make our rounds a couple of times a year. And I do love the cacophonous noise created by the voices of excited diners bouncing off distressed brick walls and the sound of plates being banged around in open kitchens. I do. But, it's always a refreshing pleasure to come to this sophisticated upscale eatery offering a menu of French haute cuisine in a subdued and elegant atmosphere for

decades. It's in a high-end residential area, so even the streets are quiet. No noisy bustle here. My Favorites: Grilled Filet Mignon; Scallops that will melt in your mouth are always a winner here; Roasted Duck Breast paired with pan seared foie gras. Creative cocktails. Reservations recommended.

SOTTO SOTTO RISTORANTE
120 Avenue Rd, Toronto, 416-962-0011
www.sottosotto.ca
CUISINE: Italian
DRINKS: Full Bar
SERVING: Lunch & Dinner
PRICE RANGE: $$$$
NEIGHBORHOOD: The Annex
This upscale restaurant offers a romantic atmosphere and a menu of traditional Italian fare. Menu favorites include: Capellini Nazini (Angel hair pasta) and Papparoelle dei castelli (egg noodles with mushrooms).

TAVERNE BERNHARDT'S
202 Dovercourt Rd, Toronto, 416-530-0008
https://bernhardtstoronto.com/
CUISINE: French Bistro
DRINKS: Full Bar
SERVING: Dinner; Closed Mon & Tues
PRICE RANGE: $$
NEIGHBORHOOD: Beaconsfield Village/West Toronto
Located in a quiet residential neighborhood, this intimate eatery specializes in rotisserie birds and locally sourced dishes. Rotisserie Chicken is the star here but they serve lots of veggies and side dishes. Reservations recommended.

TEA N BANNOCK
1294 Gerrard St E, Toronto, 416-220-2915
www.teanbannock.ca

CUISINE: American/Canadian
DRINKS: Full Bar
SERVING: Lunch & Dinner; closed Sun & Mon
PRICE RANGE: $$
NEIGHBORHOOD: Leslieville
Casual eatery featuring Aboriginal dishes, including buffalo, elk, pan-fried pickerel, and Indian tacos. Try the hominy corn soup flavored with pork. Outstanding. Nice relaxing vibe with aboriginal music playing (which is something I'd never heard, really). The name is this place, in local slang, means "friendly chat."

TERRONI
1095 Yonge St, Toronto, 416-925-4020
www.terroni.ca
CUISINE: Italian
DRINKS: Full Bar
SERVING: Lunch & Dinner
PRICE RANGE: $$$

NEIGHBORHOOD: Deer Park
This restaurant has multiple floors and a large rooftop patio. They cook outdoors on the BBQ grill when weather permits. Favorites include: Rigatoni arcobaleno and Spaghetti al Limone. Good pizzas also. Save room for the Budino di Caramello - salted caramel butterscotch pudding. Reservations recommended.

TOCA
RITZ-CARLTON TORONTO
181 Wellington St W, Toronto, 416-572-8008
www.tocarestaurant.ca
CUISINE: Canadian
DRINKS: Full Bar
SERVING: Breakfast, Lunch & Dinner

PRICE RANGE: $$$$
NEIGHBORHOOD: Entertainment District
Located in the Ritz-Carlton, this eatery offers a menu of Mediterranean & Canadian cuisine. This is a dining experience complete with a cheese cave and a pastry corridor. Menu favorites include: Octopus salad and Braised Lamb shank.

TRATTORIA MERCATTO
220 Yonge St, Toronto, 647-352-3390
www.trattoriamercatto.ca
CUISINE: Italian
DRINKS: Full Bar
SERVING: Dinner
PRICE RANGE: $$
NEIGHBORHOOD: Downtown Core
Located inside the Eaton Centre, this modern eatery offers a menu of classic Italian fare. Favorites include: Pan seared scallops with pistachio and

Polpette veal and pork meatballs. Great place to take a large group. Patio seating when weather permits.

TOFU VILLAGE
681 Bloor St W, Toronto, 647-345-3836
www.tofuvillagetoronto.com
CUISINE: Korean
DRINKS: Beer & Wine Only
SERVING: Dinner
PRICE RANGE: $
NEIGHBORHOOD: Seaton Village
This small restaurant specializes in tofu Korean dishes. Favorites include Banchan and Kimchi.

TUTTI MATTI
364 Adelaide Street W, Toronto, 416-597-8839
http://tuttimatti.com/
CUISINE: Tuscan
DRINKS: Full Bar
SERVING: Lunch & Dinner, Dinner only Sat; Closed Sun
PRICE RANGE: $$$
NEIGHBORHOOD: Entertainment District, Downtown Core
Intimate eatery offering a menu of classic Tuscan cuisine cooked by a woman who worked for years in Montalcino, a hill town a few miles from Siena. But she's been here for more than 20 years serving up family-style food that is hearty, not precious. This is why I keep coming back—there's no pretention here. They treat me (like all their regulars) like family. My Favorites: Pappardelle (braised brisket in succulent

juices served over the house made pasta); or topped with wild boar ragu; Porchetta Pizza comes sizzling hot from the wood-fired oven. Italian inspired desserts like Ricotta cake. Impressive wine list. Takeout menu. By the way, "tutti matti" means "we're all crazy." And aren't we?

VATICANO RESTAURANT
25 Bellair St, Toronto, 1 416-924-4967
www.vaticano.ca
CUISINE: Italian
DRINKS: Full Bar
SERVING: Dinner
PRICE RANGE: $$$
NEIGHBORHOOD: Yorkville
This ristorante offers a menu of traditional Italian fare. Favorites include: Penne Arribatta and Beef Carpaccio. Nice wine list. Save room for their delicious tiramisu.

WANDA'S PIE IN THE SKY
287 Augusta Ave, Toronto, 416-236-7585
www.wandaspieinthesky.com
CUISINE: Bakery/Sandwiches
DRINKS: Full Bar
SERVING: Breakfast, Lunch & Dinner
PRICE RANGE: $$

NEIGHBORHOOD: Kensington Market
This is definitely the spot for pie lovers. They offer a variety of vegetarian lunches and of course an amazing selection of pies. Favorites include the Coconut extreme experience and strawberry rhubarb. They also offer cupcakes.

INDEX

V

W

NOTES

NOTES

www.ingramcontent.com/pod-product-compliance
Ingram Content Group UK Ltd.
Pitfield, Milton Keynes, MK11 3LW, UK
UKHW021931200726
13853UKWH00010B/57

9 798201 571870